PETRONAS

TINA SHAW

Published by Pearson Education Limited, Edinburgh Gate, Harlow, Essex, CM20 2JE
Registered company number: 872828

www.pearsonschools.co.uk

First published by Pearson
a division of Pearson New Zealand Ltd
67 Apollo Drive, Rosedale, North Shore 0632, New Zealand
Associated companies throughout the world

Page Layout: Ruby-Anne Fenning
Cover Design and Illustrations: Sarah Healey

First published 2009
This edition published 2012

22
13

British Library Cataloguing in Publication Data
A catalogue record for this book is available from the British Library

ISBN 978-0-43507-619-1

Printed and bound in Great Britain

Acknowledgements
We would like to thank the children and teachers of Bangor Central Integrated Primary School, NI; Bishop Henderson C of E Primary School, Somerset; Brookside Community Primary School, Somerset; Cheddington Combined School, Buckinghamshire; Cofton Primary School, Birmingham; Dair House Independent School, Buckinghamshire; Deal Parochial School, Kent; Lawthorn Primary School, North Ayrshire; Newbold Riverside Primary School, Rugby and Windmill Primary School, Oxford for their invaluable help in the development and trialling of the Bug Club resources.

Every effort has been made to contact copyright holders of material reproduced in this book. Any omissions will be rectified in subsequent printings if notice is given to the publishers.

A division of Pearson New Zealand Ltd

CONTENTS

Chapter 1	5
Chapter 2	14
Chapter 3	22
Chapter 4	31
Chapter 5	41
Chapter 6	52
Chapter 7	58
Chapter 8	65
Chapter 9	74
Chapter 10	87
Chapter 11	97
Chapter 12	107
Chapter 13	113
Chapter 14	128

chapter one

Water! It was all they seemed to talk about: how to find it, the likeliest places for a seep, the best way to extract water from a cactus. Baba was sick of hearing about it.

The straggly group of nomads – women, men, old folk, children, their goats and rotobeasts – had been walking for the last two days. As usual, Baba, in her golden robes and fluttering red scarf, was leading the way. Every time she paused to look around, or just get a stone out of her sandal, somebody would invariably ask: *Is this the place, oh Baba? Will we find water here, oh Baba?*

Mostly she didn't bother answering them. It was too ridiculous. How was she – a twelve-year-old girl – supposed to find water in the desert? Just because she'd been born with the different-coloured eyes, that didn't mean she knew everything. She wished the last Baba was still alive: *he* could have led them around the desert looking for water.

When they finally reached the dry riverbed, Baba had had enough. Her feet were sore and she wanted to lie down in the shade of her nice tent.

The girl turned to face the group of nomads. Their faces, as always, looked to her for answers.

"We camp here," she said.

From a distance, the red tents of the nomads looked like a collection of earth mounds. White smoke rising into the sky told a different story. A gang of children ran around the tents, chasing a ball. One of the gangly rotobeasts lifted its head and brayed. The pen of goats nickered in the shade of a cactus.

Now the tents had been unloaded from the

sleds and pitched, the search for water could begin.

A cough sounded outside Baba's tent and the girl opened the flap. Quirt, bright-eyed and furry, was perched on her shoulder. Tulsi's father, Jad, stood there, tall in his brown robe. Baba's uncle, Ki, and another man waited further away. They all held shovels and empty water skins. Tulsi himself was just hurrying over from some errand or other.

"We are ready to search for a new seep, oh Baba," said Jad.

"All right, if we must," said the girl. She went back into the tent to fetch the water stick.

The men shuffled their feet. Jad cleared his throat. "Which way, oh Baba?"

She lifted her chin and sniffed, trying to sense the nearness of water. She was aware of them all watching her. A rock hawk hovered in the blue sky, as if eyeing all this human activity. Quirt, who had also noticed the hawk, tried to crawl under Baba's braid of hair.

Baba pointed in the direction of the hawk. It was as good as any other. "West," she said.

"Very good, oh Baba."

They set off. Baba led the way with Quirt on her shoulder. She held the split stick out in front of her – the stick that had been passed from one Baba to another for generations; the stick that found water.

The group walked around large boulders, past tall cacti and scrubby bushes. They went up a slight rise. At the top, Baba paused to look around. As far as the eye could see, there was the same thing: stones, sand, cacti. It was hot. She wanted to go back to her tent and lie down, but the men were waiting for her to continue.

Off to the right and down in a hollow, there were some bushes that looked promising. Baba headed that way. She could hear Ki behind her, muttering to himself. He was the grumpiest of her uncles.

Water, Baba thought with a sigh. To be truthful, she didn't have the gift. The last Baba – her great-uncle – could point out the right direction. He would walk slowly, holding out the stick. Sometimes the stick would do nothing and the men would return disappointed. But often the stick would start to tremble and point at the ground. The old Baba could find water where you least expected it. Sometimes it was a soft spot on the top of a hill. He could even tell how long the water in a seep would last.

Water, somebody would shout, and the men would start digging.

Yes, the old Baba had the knack. Even if the seep only lasted for a day or two.

He had tried to teach her, before he died, but it was just things about grasses and bushes, and the lay of the land. Nothing about the magic of the water stick. That was what Baba really wanted to know. How could a stick have the power to find water? And could it do anything else? But the old Baba didn't like to talk about the water stick.

And what would happen if they didn't find a seep this time? The water skins were nearly empty. It had been ages since they'd last found water. That last time, one of the old folk had spotted a green bush. All Baba had done was hold the trembling stick over the spot. They'd had water for a whole month. But that didn't have anything to do with her.

Baba herself hadn't been able to find water. She'd given up really trying. She just wasn't any good at it. Maybe there was no more water left in this stupid desert. What they needed was to find so much water they could stay in one place, like the market town, with its own spring. But that was ruled by the desert prince, and they couldn't live there.

They were nearly at the bushes, and the stick hadn't done anything. So Baba gave it a little shake.

"It moves," said Tulsi.

Yes, though it wasn't the stick that was doing the moving. Baba pointed it at the bushes.

"Of course," muttered Ki, "anybody can find a seep in a valley."

"Is there water, oh Baba?" asked Jad.

She turned to look at them. "Maybe," she said, "but not much. Try digging anyway. I'm going back to the camp." She trudged back over the rise, dragging the stick behind her.

That evening, Baba didn't feel like eating with the others. The men had come back frowning and silent. There was a cough outside her tent, and her mother appeared in the entrance.

"I've brought you something to eat," said Anda. She carried a plate to the sleeping mat where Baba was watching Quirt. The little creature was playing with a black cricket.

Baba sat up and took the plate. Her mother started to pull apart the girl's braid and brush her hair. Baba ate the stew. Neither of them said anything for a while. Then Baba asked if people were talking about her.

Anda sighed. "Dear, people would not complain. You are our Baba now, and perhaps the men will find water tomorrow."

"You're just saying that because you're my mother," the girl huffed.

Anda was smiling as she brushed the long dark hair. "Maybe, but I'm also saying it because it's true. The men usually find water in the end. Sometimes it just takes a bit longer."

Frowning, Baba put aside her plate. "I'm no good at being the Baba," she said. "It's not fair, having to do it, just because of the eyes."

"It's a great honour," soothed her mother. "You're still young. It'll get easier as you get older."

Then Baba had an awful thought. She looked at her mother with wide eyes. "I know – it's because I'm a girl! The water stick would work if Jad, or one of the other men, was using it."

"Oh, piffle," said Anda, giving the girl a gentle push so she could keep brushing. "Your great-grandmother was one of our Babas, remember? One of the *best*."

Baba did remember that. It was said that her great-grandmother could *smell* the water, even when it was deep in the ground. Even in a dust storm.

"Your grandmother, too – she could have been a Baba, except she didn't have the eyes."

Baba smiled, remembering her grandmother, remembering her long braid of silvery hair. Her grandmother knew so many songs. At night, as they sat around the fire, her grandmother would often sing. She had a song for each day of the year.

"I wish I could find water," sighed Baba.

Anda was plaiting the girl's long hair. Quirt, tired of the cricket, scuttled onto Baba's lap.

"Don't worry," said her mother. "You will."

chapter two

The girl was hiding behind a large rock. She put a hand over her black eye and stared at the wavy patch of sand nearby.

"Baba, Baba!" Tulsi was calling out in his irritating, mosquito voice.

She put her hand over her blue eye and squinted at the patch. Hmm, still wavy. Odd. She hadn't seen sand like that before. It looked like the heat waves that shimmered over the desert on a very hot afternoon.

"Baba," squawked Tulsi.

"Oh, go away," she murmured under her breath, "you stupid boy."

As if obeying her command, like the ever-faithful servant he was, Tulsi's whining voice started to recede, fading into the distance.

He was probably going back to the camp for reinforcements.

With a sigh, Baba stood up, smoothing down the front of her golden smock, and stepped towards the wavering patch of sand. All around her was the usual desert: rocks, gravel, sand, the occasional cactus or spindly tree. Overhead was the usual creamy blue sky.

One step, and the soft leather of her sandal touched the wavy sand. Nothing happened. Not that she was expecting very much to happen, but still . . . Disappointed, Baba turned around to go back to the camp herself. But now, instead of the usual rocks and sand, there was grass: long, luxurious grass.

The girl gasped. She turned around on the spot. She was standing in a field of grass that stretched away to the horizon. Not a horrid cactus in sight. And over there – what was that?

Baba shaded her eyes with her hand. White buildings.

"Ha!" she cried.

She was about to rush towards the buildings when she thought it might be a good idea to

know how to get back to the desert. Looking around, she found a trampled circle of shivering grass. That must be where she came through – like a door, of sorts. Baba whipped off her red silk scarf and looped it around a bunch of upright grass. There – she'd be able to find that again.

Baba set off at a trot, her golden tunic flapping in the breeze, the grass slapping at her soft trousers.

A blank, smooth wall of pale stone rose up from the ground ahead of her. Beyond were the roofs and windows of buildings. Panting, she slowed to a walk. She had never seen anything like it. Not even at the market town where the desert prince lived.

Who would live in such a place? What kind of people? She hoped they would be friendly. But then, she was Baba, the leader of her people – others might not have heard of her, but that didn't matter.

She was closer now – and approaching an arched entranceway. Through the arch she could see a beautiful yellow tree. Baba stood with her

hands on her hips, looking up. A single word was etched into the white stone: *Petronas*.

Baba held her breath and took a step forward. Despite herself, she was listening hard. If she heard a shout or a cry, then she would run very fast back to the desert.

But all was silent. Not even a bird sang.

The girl stepped into a large courtyard and looked up at the tree. It was so lovely. Trees like that did not grow in the desert. Now, something else caught her eye. Could it be?

Baba gasped, then laughed out loud.

It was a miracle – a dream come true.

Tulsi ran back to the camp in a panic. "She's gone, she's gone," he cried to the first person he bumped into, who happened to be Baba's aunt.

"Calm down, Tulsi," said Aunty. "Tell me what's happened."

"We were playing hide-and-seek, up there around the big rocks." The boy, his skinny frame shaking with anxiety, pointed further up the valley where enormous rocks were scattered like giant marbles. Once, many years ago, a mighty river would have flowed through here. "And now I can't find her."

Aunty patted Tulsi's shoulder. "Don't worry, she'll just be hiding."

"But I've looked everywhere," he wailed.

"What's up?" asked Jad, Tulsi's father.

"Tulsi's lost Baba," said Aunty, smiling thinly.

Jad nodded sagely. "Baba will come back when she's ready."

"Don't worry about Baba," advised Aunty. "Come and help us with the cactus."

Tulsi sighed and followed her over to the makeshift kitchen. Others were already sitting around on mats, cleaning and slicing the cactus pads. They would be cooked into a stew that night for dinner. It was one of Tulsi's favourite meals, although he didn't enjoy dealing with the prickly cactus.

He sat on the mat next to his sister, Ming. She was a year younger than Tulsi, but she was still able to clean and slice up a cactus pad in

less time than it took him just to remove the spines with a sharp knife.

Ming gave him a sideways look. "Lost her again, have you? What's that Baba done now?" she asked.

"Nothing," muttered Tulsi.

He didn't understand why some of the girls didn't like Baba. Jealous of her special treatment, he supposed. There was no chopping of cactus or gathering of herbs or milking of goats for Baba. For himself, he was proud to be her attendant. All of the Babas, stretching back through generations, had had their own attendant.

Baba's cousin, Tai, who was cutting up a cactus pad on a flat rock, laughed. "Maybe she's back in her tent, eating sweetmeats."

Tulsi blushed. She was talking about the last time he had lost Baba, only to find she had double-tracked back to the camp without him. But what if something *had* happened to her and he wasn't there to help? A snake could have bitten her, or she could have fallen into a hole and hurt her leg. It was his job to look after

Baba, though she didn't make it easy for him.

Tai jumped to her feet. She started mincing up and down, flipping a pretend scarf over her shoulder. "Look at me," she simpered. "I am the great Baba. See how beautiful I am!"

The other girls were falling over themselves laughing.

Tulsi's blush deepened. "Stop it," he muttered. "She's not like that."

But the girls just laughed harder.

Then somebody said, "Shush – she is coming!"

Ming hiccuped and hid her face in her hair.

At the edge of the camp, Baba had appeared. Had she heard them? With her chin in the air, the girl walked through the camp. She did not even look at the girls around the cooking area, but went straight towards her tent.

Tulsi hurried over. At the tent flap, he gave his usual cough. "May I enter, oh Baba?"

No reply. He crept in through the flap and knelt on the soft mat. Baba was sitting cross-legged on a cushion at the back of the tent. Quirt was nestled in her lap.

"Call the elders," she said, not looking at Tulsi. "I have found water."

chapter three

It was decided that three of the elders would go with Baba to the strange city. As Tulsi was always at Baba's side, it was a party of five who stepped, one by one, into the swirling patch of sand, then out into fertile grasslands.

They all looked around with big eyes and open mouths.

"What is this place?" whispered Tulsi.

"It's like the stories," breathed an old woman, Shant.

Jad was scratching his head, looking confused. Ki, the third elder, gazed around in silence. "What happened to the desert?" he asked.

"This way," cried Baba.

She led the way towards the white city, with Tulsi rabbiting along at her heels. The grass pattered against their legs. There was no other sound.

And there were the white, stone walls of the city. They all stopped, like Baba had the first time, and looked up to read the engraved word: *Petronas.*

"What is it?" breathed Shant.

"Where are we?" asked Jad, looking around.

"Who dwells in such a place?" Ki wondered.

"You'll see soon enough," said Baba with a grin, stepping forward.

They passed through the stone arch, their footsteps echoing, and entered a large courtyard. Buildings rose up on all sides. Blank windows gazed down at the small group. There was the large yellow tree, and, beyond the tree, running straight across the stone courtyard, was a canal filled with clear water. Baba ran over to it and lay down on her stomach, paddling her fingers in the lovely water.

"Well!" exclaimed Tulsi's father.

None of them had ever seen so much water.

Tulsi also flopped down to put his hand in the water. It was so cool, and it seemed to have a

slight current or movement. The canal stretched in both directions, disappearing between the buildings.

"How deep is it, d'you think?" asked Ki.

Jad was grinning. "Let's find out," he said and began to take off his sandals. He slid down into the canal, clothes and all. The water billowed up to his hips. Laughing, he sank down into it, held his nose and bobbed under. The others watched with open mouths. Then, with a spurt, he was out again, shaking himself like a dog.

"Water!" he cried.

As if that was their cue, the others leapt and jumped and slid into the water, splashing themselves and each other in their joy. All their troubles were over.

"But who lives here?" asked Ki.

They were all calm once more and stood around, dripping on the stone paving.

Baba held up her finger. "Follow me," she said.

Turning on her heel, she marched off,

squelching as she went. The others hurried to follow, their wet sandals slapping on the stone. They went through a narrow archway, along an alley between two buildings, then into another, smaller courtyard. There were many such courtyards. The buildings had smooth walls, many windows, open doorways. At every turn, they came back to the canal of lovely water. Looking about in wonder, they crossed small stone bridges over the water. Who had made these bridges? These buildings? What skills to do this! It made the market town, with its mud huts, look makeshift and poor.

Jad squatted at the side of the canal. "All this water," he said. "Is it from a deep spring, do you think?"

Ki stood silently behind him, also looking at the water.

"Who knows . . ." murmured Shant.

Jad stood up. "Incredible," he said.

"And look around," said Baba, "the place is deserted."

"Quite," said Ki, narrowing his eyes. He turned to Baba. "Are you sure nobody is here?

I feel watched . . ."

"There's nobody but us," crowed Baba.

She led them into one of the buildings – through an open doorway, up a flight of stone steps, through empty rooms with windows that looked down over the courtyard.

"Where *is* everybody?" asked Shant. "Where are the people who built these rooms, these fine canals?"

Baba laughed in triumph. "Gone. Who knows where – but gone. It has been abandoned."

"Nobody would willingly leave such a place," said Ki, looking out of a window, frowning. "It is very strange," he murmured.

"Who cares," said Baba. "This place is empty. It can be ours."

Tulsi's father looked thoughtful. "Ki makes a good point, oh Baba." He was obviously thinking about the water – and so much of it. They could settle here permanently, make this city their own. What a relief it would be to stop wandering around the enormous desert, always searching for water.

Her uncle turned away from the window.

"There's something I don't like about this place."

"Oh, Ki," said Shant, "you are always looking for problems. Baba has found a miracle, a gift."

"A mirage, more like," her uncle scoffed.

"Look . . ." Tulsi's father began in a reasonable tone.

But Baba didn't wait to hear any more. They could talk all they liked – in the end they'd still do what she told them. She tripped lightly back down the stairs, Tulsi shadowing her, and out of the building. Halfway across the courtyard, Tulsi tugged at her sleeve.

"Baba," he panted, hurrying to keep up. "Is this place made from magic?"

"Magic," she snorted. "You're as bad as Ki. Of course it's not magic." She slapped the wall of a building in passing. "See – solid as you or me."

Baba stopped in yet another courtyard. It was graced by a tinkling fountain with a stone base carved in the shape of a tree. The girl put her hands on her hips and gazed at a tall, handsome building that dominated the courtyard.

"That," she said with a satisfied smile, "will be my house."

That evening a cough sounded outside Baba's tent.

"Come in, Tulsi," the girl cried. "Don't hang about outside."

But it wasn't the boy who appeared through the flap.

"Mother," said Baba. "What are you doing here?"

Every Baba lived in their own tent from the age of ten. It was expected that the Baba would not need parents. Each Baba became a parent to the whole group. It was always the way. Sometimes she missed being in the family tent with her parents and the rollicky twins, so it was nice when her mother visited her.

Anda sighed and lowered herself to the mat. "Shant has been talking about this strange city you have found."

"There's nothing strange about it," said the girl with a sniff.

"A city in another world?" Her mother's dark

eyes regarded Baba with suspicion.

The girl smiled dreamily. “I always thought there must be other worlds apart from this one – and I was right.”

“Are we really going to go there?”

“Of course we are going there. It’s got lots of water. Much more even than the desert prince has got.”

“But, if that is true, why are there not people there?”

“How should I know?” muttered Baba.

“Could we not think about this move a little more?” Anda sat with her hands tightly clasped in her lap. “This . . . strange place,” she murmured, “surely we should find out more about it first. What if it is dangerous?”

Baba burst out laughing. “It’s an abandoned city,” she said. “There’s nothing dangerous about it.”

“But what of the old stories, oh Baba?” Anda’s eyes were dark with anxiety. “The old folk tell the story of a magical world ruled by a spirit . . . people are never seen again!”

The lamp flickered. Baba remembered sitting

on her grandmother's lap by the fire as the old folk told the story of a spirit who lived in a huge palace; a spirit that sucked the life out of innocent children. A chill settled on the girl, but she pushed the feeling away. "Oh, mother, don't be so superstitious."

Anda sat back on her heels. "It is late," she murmured, getting up. "Sleep well, my daughter."

Baba snuffed out her lamp and got under the blanket. Quirt settled by her head. "Old folk's stories," she murmured. All that water! It was like a dream come true. The old folk would soon forget their stories once they saw all that wonderful water.

chapter four

There was much excitement as the nomads packed up. *Water!* The word flew around the camp like a swift bird. Another world!

Sleds were tied to the patient rotobeasts, and tents were folded and put onto the sleds. The goats were roped together, while children laughed and ran around.

Baba led the way. Even her little pet, jumping around on her shoulder, seemed excited. They came to the wavy patch of sand.

"Watch me first," said Baba. "Then you can all follow."

She stepped onto the patch of sand and vanished. There were cries of astonishment and fear among the nomads left behind.

"Oh Baba! Where has she gone?"

Grinning, the girl appeared again. Quirt blinked his large eyes.

Tulsi, who had already been to the city, stepped forward. He carried two sleeping rolls on his shoulders. Would he and the heavy mats all get through? Baba held her breath. One step, two, and the boy was gone.

Children started running forwards with Shant behind them, helping Merti with the goats. Baba stood back while the others started to step into the other world.

"Once you're through," she cried, "wait for everybody else."

Anda and Baba's father, Kale, came up, each holding one of the twins. "I've never seen anything like it," exclaimed Kale.

"Just wait till you see the water," said Baba with a grin.

She watched, pleased with herself, as her parents stepped forwards and vanished. She would be the most famous Baba of them all. Even the desert prince, with his piffling spring, would be jealous of their city. But the best thing was, they didn't have to be nomads any more.

Panting under the weight of a rolled carpet, Tulsi followed Baba into her new house.

"Over there," she said, pointing to a corner of the ground-floor room. The fountain was visible through the window and the sound of falling water filled the space.

Tulsi dropped the carpet and unrolled it. Baba's bed. With her cushions, she would be just as comfortable here as in her tent. With her hands on her hips, she was looking around the room.

"I shall put a blanket, on poles, over my bed," she decided. "It'll be like a ceiling, so it is cosy at night."

"Like your tent, oh Baba," suggested Tulsi.

"Not at all like my tent," snapped the girl. "This is a house, not a tent. We are not nomads any more."

"Yes, oh Baba."

The girl turned slowly. "And over here I shall have a chair."

“A chair?” Tulsi looked puzzled. He knew what a chair was, though they always sat on mats.

“Yes, a chair. Like the desert prince at the market town – he was sitting on a chair outside his tent.” Baba was gazing around with a satisfied air. “And the walls . . .” she said.

Tulsi shuffled. “The walls, oh Baba?”

“Yes, I shall paint flowers on the walls.” She remembered the last time it had rained in the desert. The following morning, the cacti were covered in white flowers.

The boy cleared his throat. “But where will you get the paint, oh Baba?”

She would have cuffed him, except he darted out the door.

That night, the people sat for a long time around the fire.

“Who would leave such a place?” somebody asked.

“Maybe they found somewhere better,” another joked.

"As if!"

"If only the old Baba could have seen this place . . ."

"All we need now," somebody said, "are some fruit trees."

"Firewood would be good, too."

"We should explore the grasslands," Jad suggested. "Perhaps there are trees out there."

"There are no trees," grumbled Ki. "It is only grass – for as far as the eye can see."

Baba, sitting with a sleepy twin on her lap, said nothing, though she wished her uncle wouldn't be quite so grumpy. Old Fas was gently strumming his bakar. The others were quiet. Before long, the talk started up again.

"So much grass – the goats will get fat."

"Good for their milk."

"Think of the cheeses we will be able to make," said Merti.

"The rotobeasts will be content."

"Of course the rotobeasts will be content – they're used to living on rock leaves and moss."

"Bound to be rabbits in all that grass," said somebody else. "Nice, juicy rabbits. Not like the stringy hares in the desert."

Suddenly, one of the old folk spoke up. "Where are the stars?"

The bakar fell silent as Baba looked up. It was true. The sky was black. Not a single star shone in the darkness.

"No moon, either," muttered somebody else. "No wonder it's so dark here!"

"It's just a cloudy night," said Baba.

Nobody said anything. It was a different world, after all. They couldn't expect things to be the same as in the desert.

Baba picked up her lamp. It was late, and she was tired. Even though she was a bit nervous about going to her new house in the dark by herself, she wasn't going to show it. She wished the group good night and walked away.

The further Baba went from the fire and the soft mutter of voices, the darker it seemed to get. She trailed her fingertips along a wall to feel where she was going. The buildings loomed dark above her. And what was that sound behind her?

A patter of hurrying footsteps.

Baba whirled around. "Who is there?" she

cried, holding up the lamp.

"Only me, oh Baba." Tulsi, of course – who else? "You forgot your scarf."

She took the scarf from Tulsi. Secretly, she was relieved to see him. "Come on then. You can sleep in my house. I have many rooms."

"Very well, oh Baba." Little did she know it, but that was exactly what Tulsi had planned to do.

Next morning, peals of laughter were coming from outside as Baba hurried to the door. Three of the smaller children were skipping around the fountain, giggling. "Oh Baba, come and see what we have found." They rushed off before she could quiz them. Irritably, the girl followed.

"It can't be anything important," she muttered to Tulsi who was jogging along at her side, "or I would have discovered it already."

"Yes, oh Baba."

They walked quickly through narrow alleyways, past high buildings, through other courtyards.

"It's probably some silly thing like a centipede climbing up a wall."

"Yes, oh Baba."

They marched over a flat stone bridge across the canal. The water below them rippled as if with laughter. Up ahead, they saw the children disappearing around a corner.

"We may as well have a look, at any rate."

"Yes, oh . . ."

They turned the corner and both Tulsi and Baba came to a sudden halt.

Ahead of them, the children were dancing with glee. "See, oh Baba," one of them cried.

The large courtyard was filled with tall, airy trees, all of them dripping with yellow fruit. And the grass below them – so green, so thick! No wonder the children were giggling madly.

"I'm sure this wasn't here before," muttered Tulsi. He had already explored much of the city. "Did I miss it somehow?"

Baba also looked puzzled. She turned around on the spot, trying to see something familiar.

Sliding off her sandals, Baba stepped onto the grass. Oh, it felt so cool and soft, and sort of

ticklish. It made her want to laugh and shout. And the fruit! Baba reached up and plucked one of the small yellow fruit. It smelt like a sweet perfume and, when she bit into it, her mouth filled with succulent juice.

Behind her, Tulsi had also taken off his sandals. "Like a dream," he muttered.

Grinning, she plucked another fruit and offered it to the boy.

"Not for me, oh Baba," he said, frowning.

"Why, what's the matter? Do you think it's magic fruit?" she scoffed.

Tulsi rubbed his feet in the grass and said nothing.

Baba called to the children. "How did you find this place?"

"A bird," cried the smallest.

"We followed it," said another.

"A big yellow bird."

"And where is this bird now?" asked Baba.

The children paused, looking up at the trees. "It has gone, oh Baba," said one.

"Ah," said Baba knowingly. "So that's how it happened." She winked at Tulsi. "A bird," she

scoffed, slipping on her sandals. "I shall call a meeting and tell the people what I have found."

Tulsi hurried to put on his own sandals. "Yes, oh Baba."

chapter five

On the second night, there was a feast to celebrate the group's good fortune. Already, families and couples had moved into the houses and made them comfortable. The elders had chosen a large room in one of the buildings to be a meeting area. Here, they decided, the group could share meals and hold talks, and tonight they would have their feast.

Flatbread had been baked and cactus pads, brought from the desert, were roasted. There was even meat, and the spicy aroma filled the air. The nomads filled their cups from jugs of water and sipped at the precious liquid as if it were fine wine.

"No more musty old cactus water," said somebody with a delighted laugh.

Old Fas strummed a lively tune on his bakar.

Then Baba brought out a basket filled with the yellow fruit. There were sighs of admiration as the basket was passed around and people bit into the sweet flesh.

Shant got to her feet. "This truly is a place of bounty," she said. "Everything we need is here – and more."

People clapped and hooted. Across the room, Anda and Kale looked proud.

Everybody is happy now, thought Baba, and all because of me. If they had listened to the old folk, they'd still be in the desert, drinking bad water. As if her thoughts had been heard, Tulsi's father stood up next. "A toast," he said, lifting his cup. "To Baba, who led us to water."

"To Baba," the people cried, and the room rang with their voices.

Baba smiled, glowing with pride. She would be remembered in their people's history as the most famous of all the Babas. In centuries to come, they would still be talking about her.

Ki, however, was frowning. He was sitting

away from the fire, knees drawn up to his chest. When the basket of fruit reached him, he shook his head and passed it on. Tulsi also held back. Silly boy, thought Baba. Those two were the same – not happy unless they had something to worry about. Well, *she* wasn't worried. Smiling, Baba bit into the delicious fruit.

The people made themselves at home in the stone city. Clothes were washed, then hung out to dry. A gentle breeze flickered between the buildings, setting the bright fabrics flapping. This truly is a fine place, they said, where a breeze is sent to dry the washing.

Baba and the elders talked about making a garden. They could grow vegetables and herbs.

The goats were corralled in a small courtyard and Merti took them out each day to graze in the grasslands. The chickens were set free under the fruit trees. Outside the city, Tulsi's father herded the brown rotobeasts and they bowed their long necks to pull and chew at the green grasses. The

looms were set up in a building that became the weaving house. Tents were folded and put away. Children played in the canals, splashing and laughing.

Tulsi took to the water quickly, as if he'd spent his life by a river, instead of in the desert. The things you could do! If you took a deep breath, you could sink under and touch the bottom. Or you could lie on the water as if lying on a mat. Best of all, if you used your arms and legs, you could crawl through the water.

Old folk stopped what they were doing to watch the boy. Soon Ming had joined him and brother and sister spent hours playing around the canals. They raced each other from one bridge to another. They did handstands in the water and dived for stones.

After a few days, Baba came to find Tulsi and stood tapping her foot as she watched him playing in the canal.

"Where have you *been*?" she demanded when he came up for air. "I haven't seen you for ages."

Sheepishly, the boy hauled himself up onto the stone. "Playing in the water, oh Baba."

"Playing in the water," she scoffed. "You're supposed to be looking after me." The girl sounded hurt – and was that the sparkle of a tear in her eye?

"I'm sorry, oh Baba. It seems so safe here, and I forgot . . ."

"Forgot?" she spluttered. "You forgot?" And she marched away, clearly furious.

Ming was floating in the water, watching. "You don't have to do everything she says, you know."

Dripping and red-faced, Tulsi was already struggling into his sandals and outer tunic. "It's not like that," he muttered.

"She's just a bully," cried Ming, standing up in the shallow water.

"I am her attendant," said Tulsi softly. "Every Baba has an attendant. It is my duty." With those words, Tulsi left his sister and followed after Baba.

Tulsi still found plenty of time to slip away and explore Petronas, however. He took a piece of charcoal with him and marked the walls with a cross to show where he had been.

Eventually, he came to the other side of the city. It wasn't so big after all, thought Tulsi. There was an archway in the outer wall here, too, and he stood looking out at the endless grass. He could see two of the men in the distance. They won't find anything out there, he thought. There weren't even birds in this world.

That made him think of the bird the children had seen. Maybe they had just made it up.

Tulsi marked one side of the archway with a cross.

On his way back, Tulsi took a wrong turning. At least, he decided he must have done that, because suddenly he was in an unfamiliar alley. There was no charcoal cross, so he couldn't have come this way before. At the end of the alley was an empty courtyard. The boy turned around, trying to spot something familiar. Blank windows stared down at him. A faint humming noise came from the walls.

Tulsi ran across the courtyard and found himself in another alleyway.

Puzzled, he followed it. The alley opened into a large rectangle. Tulsi gave a low whistle. More trees! There was no fruit on them like the other trees. He went up to one and pulled on a low branch. It broke off easily. Dry twigs were scattered on the ground.

Firewood, thought Tulsi. The others would be pleased. Wasn't that what somebody had said they wanted on that first night? At any rate, it would save them burning dried rotobeast dung.

He ought to be pleased himself for finding these trees, but, instead, Tulsi felt uneasy – as if something bad was about to happen.

Tulsi and Baba were sitting under the yellow tree, watching the girls playing in the water. Tai shook her long wet hair, her robe streaming with water. Two little ones, sitting on the dry stone, shrieked with laughter as they got splashed. Ming laughed, too, and hit the water to splash them properly. Soon there was a water fight on. The little ones ran back and forth, shouting with glee. Water lay in shiny puddles on the paving.

"Look at that," said Baba. "There's so much water, it can be wasted." She thought of the market town, where the water was measured out in cups and water skins.

"What will you do, oh Baba," asked Tulsi, "now that you don't have to find water any more?"

"Hmm, good question."

The girl narrowed her eyes, thinking. Sunlight fell on the stone, making everything bright. The others were leaving the courtyard, chasing the little ones ahead of them.

"I should like to learn how to crawl through the water – like you."

Tulsi grinned. "Really, oh Baba?"

"Yes," she said, getting up, "and you are going to teach me." She pulled her outer tunic over her head and strode over to the canal.

"Wait, oh Baba," called Tulsi.

But Baba had jumped straight into the water. She bobbed under and came up spluttering and coughing. Tulsi covered his mouth to hide his smile.

"What happened?" she demanded.

"Oh Baba," he said, slipping into the water. "Did you hold your breath?"

"Of course I held my breath," said the girl, still coughing. She put her hands on her hips, even though the water came up to her waist. "What do I do first?"

"Well, you could try lying on your back, like this." Tulsi lay back in the water, his robe floating around him.

Baba glared at the boy. "That's too easy."

"Well, it takes a bit of practice. You could try, oh Baba."

"Very well." The girl let herself lie back in the water and promptly sank. She came up coughing and waving her arms.

"No, no, try again, oh Baba," said Tulsi. "This time, I will hold you."

Frowning, Baba lowered herself slowly backwards. Having Tulsi's hands under her back made all the difference. She held out her arms and gently swished the water at her sides.

"You see, the water holds you up," said Tulsi.

Baba closed her eyes. "Ah, who would have

thought water could do this . . ."

The girl barely noticed when Tulsi carefully took away his hands. Realising she was now floating by herself, Baba's eyes flew open. "Wait!" Instantly, she sank.

Tulsi couldn't help laughing.

Baba stood up and told him to be quiet. "You do not laugh at the Baba!"

"No, oh Baba," he gasped.

"You must show me how to do the water crawling now."

"Yes, oh Baba," said Tulsi, taking a deep breath. "First of all, you must put your arms out, like this." He looked like a sand cat, slinking over the sand on its belly. "At the same time, you kick with your legs and push forward. Watch me." He moved away from her, turned, and came back.

Now it was Baba's turn to laugh.

"You try," he said.

But, when she tried, the girl only managed to splash water everywhere.

"Make it smoother," cried Tulsi.

He jumped up onto the paving beside the

canal and made the arm motions. It wasn't long before Baba, glancing up at the boy, could do the same. Though her legs were kicking more like a dak than a sand cat, she was able to pull herself along in the water.

"Look," she cried, "I am water crawling."

Laughter suddenly burst out from a window overlooking the canal. Baba's sharp-eyed cousin, Tai, had been watching them. Now, slapping a hand over her mouth, the girl vanished from the window.

Baba hauled herself out of the water.

"I am a joke," she muttered, dripping.

"No, oh Baba," said Tulsi quickly. "Never that."

But she hadn't heard him. With her head down, Baba marched away.

chapter six

Somebody coughed outside Baba's house. Even though they were no longer living in tents, the old ways still persisted.

"Yes, come in," called Baba from her mat. She was dangling some yarn in front of Quirt.

Ming appeared in the doorway.

"Hello, Ming. What is it?"

"Oh Baba, have you seen Tai?"

"Why should I have seen her?"

The girl shrugged. "I've asked everyone else."

Baba felt a pang. Once Ming would have come to *her* first. They used to be friends, after all. When they were little, she and Ming always played together. Things had changed since she became the Baba.

"I've looked everywhere," said Ming, "and I

can't find her. We were going to go out into the grasslands and look for wild flowers."

Baba scratched Quirt's golden fur. "Well, maybe she's had a fight with Aunty and run off. She's done that before."

Ming frowned. "Maybe." She was looking curiously around the room. The sound of tinkling water came from outside. "This is a big house, oh Baba," she said. "Much bigger than ours."

"Yes, it is a nice house," said Baba. She picked up Quirt and started towards the door, as if she had other, more important things to do. "Anyway, don't worry about Tai. She'll turn up when she's stopped sulking."

That evening, when the group had settled around the fire to eat, Tai's mother stood up.

"I have not seen my daughter all day," said Aunty, wringing her hands. "Has anybody seen Tai?"

One of the old folk spoke up. "I saw her

yesterday, gathering firewood."

Two children stood, holding hands. "She helped change our tunics," said one.

"We were all wet," giggled the other.

Aunty looked hopeful. "Today?"

The girls looked at each other, then shook their heads.

"Aunty," said Baba, putting aside her plate. "When did *you* last see Tai?"

Her aunt wiped away tears. "Last night," she moaned. "After the meal. She said she wanted to pick some of the fruit before going to bed."

Uneasy murmurs ran around the group. It was unheard of for somebody to be missing for so long. Where could she have gone? Tai might run away to sulk, thought Baba, but she would get bored soon enough. She wouldn't stay away for a whole day.

It was Ki who spoke next. "Tell us, oh Baba, what to do." His look was challenging, as if he expected her to fail – or wanted her to.

Baba got to her feet. "Four people are to go and look for Tai," she said. "She probably hasn't gone far. She might have gone out into the

grasslands. Perhaps she has hurt herself. Split up and take a different direction each."

People were already leaving the room when Tulsi sidled up. "What does it mean, oh Baba? Where can Tai have gone?"

The girl frowned. "I don't know."

Baba was in the middle of a dream. She was galloping across the desert, like the desert prince, on a swift horse. Her red scarf flew behind her like a banner. Her hair streamed loose in the wind. The horse's hooves drummed over the hard desert sand.

"Baba!" came an annoying voice.

"Urrgh," grunted Baba, rolling over.

The horse leapt smoothly over a ravine.

Somebody was shaking her shoulder. "Baba, please, wake up!"

She jerked awake. Tulsi's eyes were wide in the light of the candle he was holding. "Oh, it's you," muttered Baba, preparing to go back to sleep. "Go away."

"Baba, please," cried the boy, shaking her more violently. "It is Tai. They have found her!"

Reluctantly, Baba got up from her warm bed. She slipped on an outer tunic and her sandals and let Tulsi lead her through the alleyways and courtyards to Aunty's house. Inside, it was lit with lamps. Several people were milling around.

Seeing Baba, Aunty cried out and gripped Baba's arm. "Come, come," she said, pulling Baba into one of the rooms.

There, on her sleeping mat, was Tai, her smooth skin glowing in the soft light. She was obviously alive and breathing, but she seemed to be deeply asleep.

"We found her like this," said Baba's uncle in a low voice. "She was lying on the ground, in the eastern part of the city."

Baba knelt beside her cousin and lifted her wrist. It was heavy and limp. The girl's pulse beat slow and steady. Baba let the arm drop and rolled back one of Tai's eyelids. The white of her eye was showing.

"Has she been injured? Was there any blood?"

"None that we could see, oh Baba."

There were often accidents and illnesses in the desert, but Baba didn't know how to deal with this. The old folk knew about healing herbs, but it was the Baba who was supposed to make the decisions.

Baba stood up, her mind racing. "I don't think there is anything we can do right now," she said slowly. "Let's wait until morning. Perhaps Tai will have woken up by then." There were murmurs of agreement. "I will look at her again in the morning."

chapter seven

The next day, Baba walked over to Aunty's house. The morning was bright and clear, and the walls of the buildings seemed to hum in the sunlight. A shadow passed overhead. Was it a bird? When Baba looked up, the sky was empty.

Aunty was sitting outside her house. She leapt up when she saw Baba.

"Oh Baba," she cried. "There has been no change."

"I will go in and see."

Aunty followed her into the house. At the doorway to Tai's room, Baba said, "Aunty, could you please fetch me a cup of water?"

"Of course, oh Baba." Her aunt hurried away.

Baba didn't want any water, but she did want

a few minutes alone with her cousin. She went into the room and sat down on the mat beside Tai. It was true; she was unchanged.

"Tai?" said Baba. The only sound was the girl's soft breathing. "Tai, it's me, Baba." The girl did not respond. What had she expected – that the girl would wake up when she spoke to her? She and Tai didn't even get on.

Baba picked up her cousin's hand. Tai wasn't faking it, that was for sure. This was no trick, no game. She studied her cousin carefully. There was no sign of injury, so she had not been attacked by a wild animal. When little Herri was attacked that time by a sand cat, he was covered in blood and scratches. There were no marks at all on Tai.

Could it be some kind of poison?

Aunty said Tai was going to pick fruit. Yet they had all eaten the fruit, and nobody else had fallen sick. But what if Tai had found another kind of fruit and eaten it?

Something else was puzzling her. If Tai had gone to pick fruit, then why was she found in the eastern part of the city? The fruit trees were in the opposite direction.

Baba laid the girl's hand back on the blanket. First, she would go and inspect the fruit trees. She might find some clue to Tai's strange sickness there.

As she stepped out of the house, Baba lifted her head, listening. She heard a faint sound, like wind over rocks in the desert. But there was no wind here. And why did it sound like laughter? Baba shook her head and carried on.

Beneath the fruit trees, Baba found a basket lying in the grass. She picked it up and stood thinking. There was fruit lying in the grass. Plenty more hung from the branches of the trees. Who *had* lived in this place before? Did they plant these trees? What kind of people were they?

If only old Baba was here – he would have known what to do about these mysterious happenings. She remembered the time he saved a rotobeast from going into the quicksand.

Baba sighed and sat down. It was so pleasant

here. She lay back in the grass and closed her eyes. So sleepy . . . She could just drift off to sleep.

The sound of wings cut through the air and Baba opened her eyes. The sky was empty. Yet she was sure she'd heard . . . what? A bird?

The girl sat up, shaking her head. She had to get back.

When Baba got back to her house, Tulsi was sitting outside in the sun, playing with Quirt. The boy jumped up when he saw her. Baba's pet ran up her tunic and onto her shoulder.

"Oh Baba, I have found something," said Tulsi.

"What now?" she asked, stroking Quirt's soft fur. The little creature was quivering, as if he was also worried about Tai.

"Let me show you."

They walked through the city, their sandals slapping quietly on stone. There was a smell of smoke on the air. People were baking flatbreads.

Tulsi led the way back to the main courtyard, past the yellow tree and into an alleyway on the other side. Beyond it was an open space filled with long grass. Flowers sprang up from the grass.

"Oh," exclaimed Baba. "Flowers!"

The only flowers any of them had seen were cactus flowers, and they were white, but these flowers were of many different colours, like the gems she had seen traded at the market.

Baba waded through the grass, snapping off the long stems of flowers as she went and gathering the blooms. "No need for paint now," she said. "I shall put *real* flowers all around my house." When her arms were full, she bent down to smell the brightly hued blooms. "And the perfume – so sweet."

She turned back to Tulsi, her face glowing, Quirt chittering on her shoulder. "Come on, we'll put them in my house."

Suddenly, something flashed through the grass. Baba jumped. "What was that?"

"Look!"

A rabbit was streaking away.

"Ha," cried Baba. "Wait till I tell Ki about that." She was moving away now. "That'll cheer him up."

"But, oh Baba . . . " the boy murmured.

She looked back, still thinking about the rabbit.

"This wasn't here before," said Tulsi.

"What do you mean?"

"This," said the boy, waving his hand at the flowers. "Two days ago, the city wall was here." He pointed back the way they had come. "My mark is back there – we passed it already. This is new."

Baba looked at the flowers in her arms. They were as real as her growing hunger. She could smell them. The grass – she bent over and pulled up a blade. It was as real and juicy as the yellow fruit. And the rabbit . . .

"How can it be new?"

"I don't know," said Tulsi, "but it wasn't here before. No flowers. No grass."

Baba shook her head. "It's not possible. You must be mistaken."

"I know what I know," he said quietly.

"You're as bad as the old folk," said Baba, "with their spirit stories."

chapter eight

Next, a young man went missing. It was Merti, who tended the goats.

"He went out last night," said his mother, "to check on the goats. He said they were restless. He could hear them bleating. I fell asleep, and the next morning, he wasn't here."

Baba listened as Merti's mother continued her story. At first she had thought her son had got up early to take the goats out into the grasslands. Merti often got up early. It didn't seem unusual. "But then I saw that the goats were still here."

Baba and the others went around to the goats' enclosure, where Shant was feeding them some cut grass. "Have you found Merti yet?" she asked.

"No," said Baba. "You haven't seen him?"

"Not I," said the old woman.

"What if he knocked his head and fell in the water?" cried Merti's mother. "Or he could be lying injured somewhere!"

"He's probably all right," said Baba. She wasn't so sure about that, but she didn't want people to panic.

Merti's mother wiped away her tears. "And who is going to take the goats out?"

A voice spoke up. "I will." It was Baba's father, Kale. He was holding one of the twins by the hand. Behind him, Baba could see curious faces peering at the goats.

"What has happened?" somebody asked.

"It is the sickness again," said another.

Ki walked up. "What is it?" he said, frowning.

"Nothing," said Baba quickly. "But Jad will lead another search party. Merti did not come back last night."

The group was quiet that evening at the meal. Fas didn't play his bakar, and Aunty stared grimly into the distance. When Jad came in, everybody looked up. Merti's mother ran forward. "Have

you found him? Have you found my son?"

Jad nodded. "He was in the eastern part of the city."

Murmurs filled the room. *What was he doing there? Just like Tai!*

Baba and some others hurried to Merti's house. Just like Tai, he showed no sign of a mark or injury. His face was pale, as if carved from stone, and he seemed to be in a deep sleep. Baba stood looking down at the young man as the others gathered behind her, muttering. Aunty was there, her face grimmer than ever. Tai could be explained away, thought Baba, even though the girl still hadn't woken up. But another one?

A sickness, maybe. But what kind of sickness made people fall into a deep sleep?

CHAPTER 8

That night, Baba dreamed again of riding a horse. She was the desert prince. The horse was galloping fast across the sand, and she laughed out loud. But then something changed. She seemed to be in the sky. The horse stumbled. She was tumbling, falling. Everything was moving very slowly. She was looking down at Petronas – its white roofs and maze of alleyways – and there was Merti, lying on the ground. Baba gasped. Perched on his chest was a huge yellow bird. It looked up at Baba and winked one black eye.

She woke to the distant sound of laughter.

Somebody coughed at her door. "Come in," called Baba from her mat.

"You are not up yet, daughter," said Anda.

"I didn't sleep well."

Her mother sat beside her. "I didn't, either, and the twins were restless all night." She smoothed a hand over Baba's hair. "Sit up, oh Baba, and I'll brush your hair."

Baba sat up, rubbing her eyes as her mother began brushing her hair.

"Actually, I've got other news."

"What? Has somebody else gone missing?"

"No, no," soothed Anda. "It is Ki. I'm worried about him."

"Oh, Ki," said Baba, then winced as her mother jerked the brush roughly through her hair. "You are pulling too hard."

"Last night, he and some others were talking around the fire. I had come out to get a piece of flatbread for the twins. They stopped talking when they saw me."

"So?"

"I don't like it. Secrets. People whispering. It is not our way, not the desert way, to have secrets."

Baba turned to look at her mother. "What can *I* do about that?"

"You could try talking to him," said Anda. "Find out what is bothering him."

"I'll see." She got up, reaching for her outer tunic. Ki's moods didn't seem very important at the moment.

Anda, however, still looked worried. "Promise me you will talk to Ki."

"Yes, yes, mother. Now I must go and wash."

"Of course, oh Baba."

Tulsi went exploring again. There was something about Petronas he didn't like. Something secret.

If he kept looking, he thought, maybe he would find it.

Wandering past a shadowy corner, he spotted something – a mark on the wall like a . . . He looked closer. It was a footprint. He looked up. At the top of the high wall were two sticks tied together. What was it?

Tulsi went outside the city wall and followed it around to the right. This was where he had seen the sticks. But, on this side of the wall, there was a long, knotted rope hanging down. So that explained the sticks. They were holding the rope in place, like a ladder. Somebody had thrown the sticks up there to hook them on to the top of the wall. He gave the rope a tug. It was strong. But what was the point? Anybody could just walk into Petronas. You didn't have to climb the wall.

The boy pulled on the rope with both hands. The sticks made a good anchor. He put one foot on the wall, then the other, and hauled himself up onto the first knot.

Tulsi looked back at the ground, then up at the high wall. Hey ho, up we go.

In a few moments, he was sitting on top of the wall, grinning. Phew, so high! He could see into the top-floor windows. It felt fantastic to look down on everything and see so far. Shading his eyes, he looked out over the city. It was bigger then he had thought it was.

But what was that?

It looked like the top of a tower. Tulsi made a note of the direction so he could find it later. Then he looked more closely at the sticks. One was a branch. The other was a good, strong stick; a walking stick, in fact. It was old and weathered. How long had it been up here? A carved snake curled around the stick. There were snakes like that in the desert. They were tasty, roasted over the fire. He hadn't seen any snakes since coming to Petronas. Not even basking in the sun.

Tulsi ran his hand over the snake. What was the stick doing here? Had other desert people once come to Petronas?

He kicked his heels against the wall and stared out over the empty grasslands.

The sun was going down, and the city was filling with long shadows. Tired of all the talk around the fire, Baba was heading back to her house when a movement flickered at the corner of her eye. She glanced over her shoulder, but there was nothing there. Not even faithful Tulsi. She hurried on. Then another movement – something *was* there.

Baba stopped, squinting in the dim light.

One of the shadows moved. It detached itself from the wall like a cloud, a patch of mist.

"Who are you?" she demanded, her voice shaking. Where was Tulsi when she needed him?

The shadow became a bird, grey and dim. It rose a little way into the air, as if testing its wings, then flapped away.

"Wait," cried Baba, hurrying after it.

She could hear the sound of its wings up ahead. At each corner, the bird flew ahead, disappearing out of sight just before she could catch it.

Baba ran after it. There was its tail, flicking around another corner. There it was, swooping across an empty courtyard. Always just out of

reach. Where was it going?

"Stop," cried Baba, puffing with the effort.

The bird slowed, as if it had heard her, and landed on a low wall. They were in a grassy place Baba hadn't seen before. A tower rose out of the shadows nearby. Was she in the eastern part of the city? Suddenly, Baba was afraid. She drew back against the wall of a building. Was this what had happened to Tai and Merti? Did they also follow the bird?

The bird's yellow eyes were fixed on Baba. Slowly, it spread its huge wings. For a moment, she felt hypnotised.

Run! thought Baba. She turned and fled.

chapter nine

Baba ran to her parents' house. Kale was playing with the twins on the mat in the main room. "Daughter, what is the matter?" he asked.

Baba sat down on the mat with the twins, breathing hard. "There was a bird . . . a great big . . . I thought it was going to eat me . . ."

"Slow down. Tell me what happened."

The twins started crawling over her lap. "Baba," they squeaked.

"They are learning to talk," she said.

"Yes," said Kale. "Soon we won't be able to stop them." He leaned back against the wall. "But tell me about this bird."

Baba frowned. "It seemed to call to me. So I followed it. Before I knew it, I was in a strange part of the city. I think it wanted to . . ."

"A bird," said Kale, shaking his head. "But there are no birds here. Are you sure you didn't fall asleep and dream of a bird?"

"No," she insisted. "It was real."

"I know it must have *seemed* real," said Kale slowly, "but you know what vivid dreams you have. All the Babas have such dreams."

"It wasn't a dream," said Baba. Now her father had said it, though, she wasn't quite so sure. *Had* she gone back to her house and fallen asleep?

"Why," said her father, chuckling, "I remember your great-uncle once dreamed he'd floated up into the sky hanging onto a water skin."

"It wasn't a dream," cried Baba, jumping up. Startled, the twins stared at her with big eyes.

"Baba," said Kale, "I didn't mean to . . ."

But she was already running out of the house as the twins started bawling behind her.

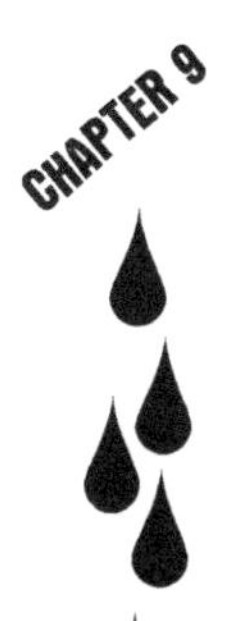

The next day, Tulsi and Baba were making their way to the meeting room when Baba noticed that the boy seemed to be in an odd mood. Was he upset about Merti?

"What are you thinking?" she asked.

Tulsi started nervously. "I think that . . . other people have been here in Petronas," he said.

Baba looked at him in surprise. "What do you mean?"

"That maybe . . ."

"What?"

Tulsi ducked his head. "Maybe, a long time ago, other desert people came here."

"Why do you say that?"

"I found something . . ."

They crossed the canal. The water looked dull and shivery. The old folks . . . was there some truth in their stories after all, wondered Baba?

"What did you find?" she asked.

"Well, it was . . ." He stopped, listening.

Baba could hear it, too. The meeting room was just ahead and the rumble of Ki's voice could be heard quite clearly.

". . . the people who built this city?" he was saying. "What if there were many people living here, but they caught a sickness. A sleeping

sickness." Now the sound of many voices murmuring in response reached them. "What if this is just the beginning?" continued Ki.

"But there have only been two," another voice said.

"Yes, two people so far," said Ki, "but how long do you want to wait? Until the sickness has taken six people, or seven? We know nothing about this place . . . What if there is something in the water?"

More murmurs.

Outside the meeting room, Baba and Tulsi glanced at each other. Baba felt the blood draining from her face.

"But we have all been drinking the water," said a voice.

"Yes, but perhaps it only affects some people – not all." Her uncle sounded so reasonable. What if they started listening to him and not to her? "How do we really know what is causing this sickness? It could be anything . . . It could be the air that we breathe."

More murmurs.

"Remember," rumbled Ki, "this is a world

we don't know. A strange world. It is not the desert."

"Not the desert," voices echoed.

"And maybe," Ki continued, "we need to think carefully about what we have to do . . ."

Baba, followed by Tulsi, stepped into the room.

"What do you mean, Uncle?" Baba asked.

"Nothing," Ki muttered, his face dark with anger.

Baba faced her people. This was her family – the people who trusted her. She stood up and looked at them with her blue eye and her black eye. "It is true that something has happened to Tai and Merti . . . but maybe it's nothing too serious. We have everything we need here – fruit, firewood, water."

"Water," they murmured.

Baba held up her hand. "Only – my uncle is right. This *is* a new place for us." Should she tell them about the bird? She shivered, remembering the look in its eyes. But what if it had been just a dream as her father suggested? No, better not to say anything about the bird just yet. "We still

need to be careful, just as we are in the desert. So, no walking around by yourself after sunset."

Ki left the room abruptly, looking sour, and others began moving, too. They gathered to prepare the meal or to talk in small groups.

Tulsi tugged at her sleeve. "Oh Baba, won't people start to be afraid now?"

"I don't think so," said Baba, "but they need to be careful."

Now, Baba seemed to hear whispers wherever she went. People were talking behind her back. She went to sit with Ming and the other girls around the fire one night. Ming and Tulsi, she had noticed, weren't playing together in the water any more and she wanted to talk to Ming about it. The girls had been chatting together, but they stopped when Baba sat down. Then Ming got up and walked off. The other girls turned away.

Secrets . . . Anda was right – it wasn't the desert way.

At least her uncle seemed to have settled down. Probably sulking, thought Baba. She remembered her mother wanted her to talk to Ki, but what could she say? He seemed to be against everything. Better to leave him be.

Baba went looking for her mother instead.

Anda was in the weaving room with two other women. When they saw Baba, the women left, casting sidelong glances as they went.

"What's wrong with them?" asked Baba, sitting on a stool next to her mother's loom.

"Take no notice," said Anda quickly. "They are easily led."

Baba watched her mother's hands moving over the loom. The shuttlecock flew back and forth, carrying the soft goat's yarn.

"It's Ki, isn't it?" she said. "Why does he fight me like this?"

Anda sighed. "It's been hard for him since the old Baba died. He finds it hard to accept . . ."

"A girl as our Baba," she finished bitterly.

Her mother shrugged. "He'll get over it."

Baba didn't think so. Ki was turning people against her – people like Ming. How long before

they started wanting to leave Petronas? If only her grandmother were here – she could have talked some sense into Ki.

"Tell me about my grandmother," said Baba.

Anda smiled. "There was this one time – I was just a little girl – when she walked into camp carrying this big, bulging sack."

"What was in it?"

"An enormous snake," said Anda. "I still remember, when it was laid out on the ground, it was longer than a rotobeast. She had killed it with a stone." Anda chuckled. "We ate well for ages after that."

"She must have been very brave."

"Oh, I don't know about that," said Anda, "but, when she came up against a problem – or a very big snake – your grandmother thought quickly, and she found a solution."

"I miss my grandmother," murmured Baba.

Anda sighed. "We all do."

"Tell me," said Baba, fiddling with a string of soft yarn, "how did my grandmother die?" Nobody had told her properly. An accident, they always said, and changed the subject.

Anda pursed her lips and glanced at her daughter. She took a deep breath and said, "Your grandmother . . . She took the water stick."

"From old Baba?"

Anda nodded. "None of us knew . . . A baby had been taken by a large sand cat. Your grandmother went after the cat."

"What happened?"

Her mother looked afraid – more scared than Baba had ever seen her. "We found her some way from the camp, stone cold. Beside her was the scorched skeleton of a sand cat."

Baba struggled to understand. "But how . . ."

"We'll never know for sure," said her mother softly.

So that was why old Baba didn't like to talk about the water stick. The girl bowed her head, overwhelmed.

There was the sound of running feet. What now, Baba wondered? Please let there not be another missing person.

Tulsi burst into the weaving room.

"Baba, please come," he cried. "Tai has woken up."

Several people were already gathered outside Aunty and Uncle's house when they arrived. Uncle grinned when he saw Baba. "You see, Tai is going to be all right," he said.

Inside the house, Aunty was kneeling beside Tai's mat. Baba knelt on the other side. Her cousin's brown eyes were open, staring blankly at the ceiling.

"Has she said anything yet?" asked Baba.

A tear fell down her aunt's face. "Not yet, oh Baba."

"But she is awake. That is good."

"Yes, oh Baba," said Aunty sadly.

Baba leaned closer to her cousin's vacant face. "Tai," she said, "can you hear me?"

Her cousin blinked.

Baba grabbed her hand. "Tai, speak to me. What happened?"

A sigh came from the girl, but nothing more.

"You see," Aunty whispered. "She does not speak. Though I did give her a little water, some broth, too, and she drank it."

"Good," said Baba, sitting back on her heels. Now what?

"Burn some herbs," she told Aunty. "Maybe that will help."

Rising to her feet, Baba looked down at Tai. Her cousin seemed to be under a spell. "And get one of the old folk to sing to her."

"Yes, oh Baba," said her aunt with a sigh.

Baba was dreaming – not of being a desert prince, or of riding a horse, but of old Baba.

They were out in the desert, looking for water. Nobody else was around. Her great-uncle was telling a story, as the old folk liked to do around the fire at night.

... *Your great-grandmother found the place*, old Baba was saying, *just as you did. It was beautiful. All the water we could use. Many good things.*

Yes, yes, said Baba impatiently, *just like Petronas.*

Old Baba looked away. *But it was more like the quicksand,* he said.

How do you mean, Uncle? asked Baba.

The old man pointed at the ground with the

water stick and Baba recognised the white crust she saw there – salt. It was something he had taught her. The salt meant quicksand.

Danger, he said.

Suddenly there was a rotobeast, bellowing. It was being sucked into the quicksand.

Uncle, cried Baba, *do something!*

Old Baba raised the water stick above his head. He looked angry. For a moment, Baba thought her great-uncle was going to hit her with the stick. She put up her hand to stop him but, instead, he brought it down hard on a rock. Sparks flew from the stick and fire leapt up. Baba ducked as a bird flew out of the flames.

The girl woke suddenly, gasping, tangled in her blanket.

Tulsi went to the eastern side of the city to have a better look at the tower. It rose up, tall and straight, with a thin window opening near the top. Tulsi wondered why it had been built. As a lookout? But there was nothing out there to see, and it didn't look like the kind of place you'd want to live in.

There was an open doorway, and he peered inside. The floor was littered with straw. Stone steps rose steeply upwards, following the wall towards the top of the tower. A breeze seemed to whine up and down these steps. As curious as he was, Tulsi didn't want to go inside. The place gave him a bad feeling.

Instead, he walked slowly around the base of the tower.

Halfway around, he saw something scratched into the stone. It was a handprint. Tulsi put his own hand inside the print. It was larger than his hand, but not by much.

Somebody had been here and marked their passing. There was no way to tell how long ago. But why had they left this mark?

Tulsi dropped his hand. He wanted to get back to the others. He felt as if he was being watched, and it was so quiet here. He hurried away.

chapter ten

Shouts had woken Baba. Where was Tulsi?

She slipped on her tunic and hurried out into the night. Lights glowed in the distance and voices rose and fell. She jumped as somebody joined her. It was Shant.

"I was asleep," said the old woman.

"Me, too," said Baba. "What's going on?"

"I don't know."

Up ahead, lamplight shone from the meeting room. Shant hurried inside, but Baba lingered at the open door.

Many of their people were inside. She spotted Tulsi crouched against a wall.

"How long must we wait?" Ki was shouting. "Until all of us are asleep? Until there is nobody left to care for the sick ones?"

Jad stood up. "You don't know that will happen."

"Yes, but what if it does? Then it will be too late for us to do anything."

"Give Petronas a chance," said Jad.

One of the other men stood up. "We have given it a chance already."

"I say we go – now!" cried Ki.

Somebody else stood up. "But, Ki, how can we go when Baba has not given the word?"

"That's right!" said another. "We must trust the Baba."

"The time for trust is past," Ki shouted. "We must escape before it is too late. Who is with me?"

Baba stepped quietly inside. What would her grandmother have said? Even now, Baba didn't know. She felt so young – as if she would never be as wise as her grandmother or the old Baba.

"This is wrong," she said loudly, and the room fell silent. "We must work together."

"Oh Baba, tell us what to do," somebody cried out.

She took a deep breath. Her grandmother

wasn't here to help, and Baba could only say what *she* knew.

"It is too soon to be leaving Petronas. I think we should stay," she said.

People clapped. Sitting against the back wall, her father was nodding. Before anything else could be said, Baba hurried away.

Things seemed to settle down. There was no more talk from Ki, no more night meetings, and no more sleeping sickness. Tai was able to sit in the sun outside her house now. Even Merti was starting to look brighter. Baba hoped that everything would be all right.

It was the twins' birthday – they were turning one. Thinking it would cheer everybody up, Anda planned a party in the courtyard outside their house. The old folk had been making twig torches to light up the courtyard. Shant and Merti's mother made honey treats from goat's cheese. Fruit was gathered, and children wove headbands from yellow leaves. Baba picked bunches of flowers.

Anda stood in her doorway, smiling. "This is so wonderful," she said, "and the twins are so excited."

"I hope they won't get too excited," said Baba.

"They'll be fine," said Anda. "You know what else I'd like?"

"What?" Baba was pleased her mother was so happy. The party had been a good idea.

"Music," said Anda, clapping her hands. "We'll get Fas to play his bakar."

"We can have dancing, too."

"Oh, yes!"

"I'll go and find Fas," offered Baba.

But Fas was nowhere to be found. Baba looked out in the grasslands. She looked in the small house he had taken in her own courtyard. She went to the fruit trees, thinking he might be playing his bakar there.

Baba felt sick. Surely he couldn't have . . . Dragging her heels, she made her way to the eastern part of the city. It seemed different over here now, but she was still able to follow the charcoal marks Tulsi had made. At last, she

came to the stone tower.

"Oh, Fas, please don't be here," Baba whispered.

But, sure enough, when she walked around the tower, there was the old man, lying on the ground as if asleep.

Back at her parents' house, the people were gathering. The children were playing and laughing, and everybody was happy. Baba walked up to her mother.

"Have you found Fas?" asked Anda. Then she saw the look on Baba's face. "Oh, no," she whispered. "Is he . . ."

Baba nodded. "I found Fas in the eastern part of the city."

The others fell silent. Children stood around, looking serious. Ki, who had been putting up the twig torches, walked away frowning. So much for their party.

The next morning, a group of people gathered outside the entrance to the city, watching four distant figures – one of them Ki – wading through the grass, away from Petronas.

"Where are they going?" asked Baba.

"Back to the desert," sighed Shant, who stood nearby.

"But what will they do?" Baba felt like crying. "They haven't even taken a goat. All they have is their mats and one tent between them."

The old woman sniffed. "They have some crazy plan of living at the market town."

Somebody laughed. "Good luck to them."

Everybody knew that the desert prince didn't welcome strangers to the heavily guarded town. There was only so much water to go around. It was fine to go there for the day and trade, but that was all.

"This is your fault!" Ming stood, her hands on her hips, eyes flashing.

"Hush, Ming," said Shant.

"It's true," cried the girl. "If it wasn't for Baba, Tai would be all right and the others wouldn't be leaving."

"Ming, you are being . . . "

"I don't want to hear," sobbed the girl and

ran away from them.

Baba put her scarf over her head. "We have always stayed together," she said sadly. "It is the desert way. Now look what has happened."

Shant squeezed her arm. "Ki will come to his senses. They will come back."

Baba looked at the kindly old woman. "I hope you are right." It didn't make her feel any better, though. She had to talk to her mother. People were going back to their chores, but Anda wasn't among them.

"Where is my mother?" she asked.

"She went to get more wood," said Shant. "Last night, after the meal."

Her mother hadn't been at the morning meal, either. Baba had thought she was busy with the twins. Now, suddenly, she felt afraid. "I told everybody to be careful. Not to go walking by themselves," she said.

"Yes, but it was still light and . . ."

Baba didn't wait to hear any more. She ran to find Tulsi.

"Come on," she cried. "We have to go to the tower. We have to look for my mother."

"Why?" asked Tulsi. "What has happened?"

"I don't know."

Already Baba was running towards the eastern part of the city, with Tulsi at her heels. She didn't need to think about where to go. She knew.

They ran through empty courtyards and over bridges, past silent buildings, through the firewood trees.

"Wait," gasped the boy.

Baba stopped. "What is it? Quickly!"

Tulsi pressed a hand into his side. "This is new," he said.

The girl looked around wildly. She was desperate to find her mother, but Tulsi was right. This was something she hadn't seen before – a long walkway with pillars. On the other side was another alley. Should they go that way? But Tulsi was pointing towards the tower, which rose above the buildings to their right.

"That way," he said.

Again they ran, until at last they burst out into the open space around the tower. Everything was silent. No bird sang. No breeze blew.

Baba glanced around nervously. "Where could she be?"

"What makes you think she is here?" asked Tulsi.

"Just a feeling. Let's try over there," she added, pointing towards one of several alleyways leading away from the tower.

The walls of the alleyway seemed to crowd over them as they ran along it and out into a small grassy courtyard. Baba gasped. Her mother was lying there, as if fast asleep.

She knelt beside Anda on the grass and lifted her mother's hand to put it to her cheek. The hand felt cold. Tears ran down Baba's cheeks. She wanted to curl up here beside her.

"Wake up," she whispered.

But Anda was in a deep sleep, far from her daughter's reach.

Baba looked up at Tulsi. "What is this sickness?" she muttered.

"I don't know, oh Baba." Tulsi himself looked close to tears. After a moment, the boy cleared his throat. "We will need some help, oh Baba."

She nodded. “Go and get somebody. I will stay with my mother.”

chapter eleven

Now, more than ever, she had to get to the bottom of this mystery. So, while Kale watched over her mother, Baba went to see Merti. The young man was propped up against the wall of his house, with his mother feeding him broth from a bowl. Some of the broth went into his mouth, but most of it seemed to be running down his chin. Merti's mother wiped it away with a cloth.

"Any change yet?" asked Baba.

"He doesn't see me," moaned the woman. "Why can't he see me?"

"I don't know," replied Baba. "Does he speak?"

"During the night, he spoke in his sleep."

"What did he say?"

"Sorry, oh Baba, I could not make out the words." The woman put her hand on Baba's arm. "And now your mother?"

The girl nodded, biting back tears.

Now Baba went to see Tai. Her cousin was lying on her sleeping mat, staring at the ceiling, humming – one note, and then another, repeated over and over again. It sounded familiar, though it was nothing like the songs the old folk sang around the fire.

Baba sat cross-legged beside her cousin. "Hello, Tai," she said. "It's me, Baba."

"Oh Baba . . ." the girl said dreamily.

Aunty, standing in the doorway, gasped. "She speaks! She must be getting better."

"How do you feel?" asked Baba.

"Oh Baba," the girl sighed. Her pale fingers twisted restlessly on her chest.

"What happened, Tai?"

The girl closed her eyes. Thinking she had fallen asleep, Baba was about to go, but then Tai spoke in a low voice. Baba had to lean forward to hear the words.

"A bird," whispered the girl.

In a daze, Baba wandered around the city. She stood in the main archway and looked out at the empty grasslands, holding Quirt close, stroking the silky fur. Behind her, the yellow tree rustled, as if sharing a joke.

What *was* this place? Perhaps Tulsi was right to think it was magic. Why had she not seen it herself? Instead, she had been impulsive and brought her people here. She hadn't considered the dangers. Hadn't old Baba tried to teach her to be aware of all possible dangers? He had taught her about snakes and thorn bushes and dust storms. He hadn't taught her about worlds beyond the desert, but still she should have been more careful. Ming was right: it was all her fault.

Sadly, Baba wandered on, past the yellow tree and into the alley that led to the field of flowers.

Even the flowers seemed to mock her. Everything had seemed so perfect here in Petronas – too perfect. The old Baba would not have made such a stupid mistake. But then, she was just a girl – a twelve-year-old girl. Ki was right to leave. He was the one who ought to be leading their people, not her.

Baba slumped against the sunny wall and watched the flowers swaying in the breeze. She put Quirt on the ground and watched as the little creature started grooming himself.

"Oh Baba?"

A tinny voice was calling her name. She smiled, remembering the day she had hidden behind the rock.

"Tulsi," she called. "I am here!"

The boy's head appeared around the corner. "I was looking for you," he said, sitting down next to her in the sun.

"And now you have found me," said Baba, though kindly. She was glad Tulsi had come looking for her. Without her mother, there was nobody else she could talk to.

"What are you doing, oh Baba?"

She fiddled with the fringe of her red scarf. "Just thinking."

They sat in silence for a few minutes. A

breeze played in the long grass. Baba narrowed her eyes.

"Look at those flowers," she said. "What do you see?"

Tulsi squinted at the field. "Um, I don't know, oh Baba."

Baba looked at the boy, her blue and black eyes shining. "It hasn't changed."

"What?"

"These flowers," she said, waving her hand at the field. "Nothing has changed since we last came here. Yet surely some of these flowers should be dead by now, or going brown with age or something? But they are all exactly the same."

It was true: nothing had changed. Even the breeze rippling the grass had not changed. She picked up Quirt, who scuttled onto her shoulder.

Then Baba had another, more worrying thought.

"What if something here wants to hurt us?" she asked.

"I'm not sure," Tulsi said slowly, "but I'm worried."

"Me, too." Baba looked thoughtful. "We weren't doing so badly in the desert, really. Maybe Ki was right to go back."

"Yes, but then there is the water here."

"It was the water that got us into this mess," said Baba. True, she had found water, but it looked as if she had found something else as well. Or rather, something had found *them*.

"There is something wrong here in Petronas," said Baba. "I think we will have to leave this place and . . ."

Tulsi patted her arm to get her attention. He put a finger to his lips, then pointed at the flowers. Puzzled, Baba looked carefully. The flowers closest to them were very still and leaning towards them. Her eyes wide, Baba looked back at Tulsi. He nodded. Yes, the flowers were listening.

Tulsi was now pointing beyond the walls. He wanted to go outside the city. They both got up and started moving towards the alley. Looking back, Baba saw that the flowers were again swaying in an invisible breeze.

They went some way out from the city and flopped down in the long grass. The sky was blue and wide above them.

"How can flowers be listening to us?" wondered Baba.

"I don't know," replied Tulsi, frowning.

"Maybe even the walls can hear us."

"Sometimes . . ." the boy began hesitantly. "No, it will sound stupid."

Baba looked at him. "What? Tell me."

"Sometimes, mostly at night, I have heard humming."

"You mean like a person is humming?"

"More like the sound of a bakar when Fas is tuning it," said Tulsi, "only there is nobody there." He looked anxious. "Have you heard it, too?"

"Yes, I know what you mean." She watched Quirt batting a stalk of grass. "I didn't think anything of it, but, once you've noticed, it's always there."

"It makes me sleepy just thinking about it."

Baba looked at the boy as if seeing him for the first time. "You're right," she said slowly. "It's like the city wants us to go to sleep."

The grass rustled around them – a soothing sound. Baba made a nest of grass and put Quirt into it.

"You know, Tai was humming when I saw her last . . . It sounded a bit like that."

Tulsi frowned, but said nothing.

"There is something else about Tai," said Baba. "She spoke to me – just a few words. She said something about a bird."

The girl pulled out a length of grass and started chewing the end. She thought about how she had followed the bird through the city, and how afraid she had been. Now she told Tulsi about it.

His eyes grew large. "But what *is* this bird? Some kind of spirit?"

"I don't know." Baba shivered, even though the sun was warm.

"The children," said Tulsi suddenly. "They saw a bird."

The girl's cheeks went hot. Yes, and she had scoffed at them, but now she knew they were right. They *had* seen a bird. A yellow bird.

"So, if it's not a sickness," said Tulsi, "what is it?"

Baba shook her head. "It's as if . . . they are drained of energy. Like if you leave a bowl of water out in the desert."

"And the water gets sucked into the hot air," said Tulsi. "Can it be a bird that somehow feeds on people?"

"But I don't think it's a real bird," Baba said quickly.

"No, it's not a real bird," Tulsi agreed. "Then there is the way the city keeps getting bigger," he added.

Baba threw away the piece of grass. "Yes, it is growing." Then she had another thought. "But what about the water? If the flowers aren't real, then perhaps the water isn't real, either?"

"I don't know," said Tulsi. "It's wet. It seems real enough to me."

"The water . . . the fruit," muttered Baba.

"What?"

The girl blinked her strangely coloured eyes. “It’s as if the city knows what we need and gives it to us.” She plucked at the end of her red scarf. “What if . . . the city has laid a trap for us?”

Tulsi’s eyes were wide. “But, oh Baba, what can we do?”

She picked up Quirt. “There’s only one thing we can do,” she said.

chapter twelve

For several seconds, the group simply stared at Baba in silence. She lifted her chin and repeated what she'd just said: "We must leave this place."

Voices suddenly filled the room. *Leave? Why leave? Back to the desert? We have nice houses here. And what about the water? The water . . . water!*

Baba clapped her hands. A hush fell. "It is no longer safe here," she said. "There is something in this city, something we can't see, that means us harm. Something that looks like a bird."

"A bird?" asked a puzzled voice.

Another voice broke the brief silence: "Ki was right then."

"But, oh Baba, it was you who led us here," said somebody else.

Voices clamoured. "You found us water."

"There is fruit, firewood . . ."

"Just because your mother . . ."

"Why *should* we go back?"

"And give up all this?"

Then a single voice rose above the others: "We trusted you!"

There was a stunned silence. Baba blinked. Nearby, Tulsi was holding his breath. Even Ming's mouth fell open. Baba's father, balancing both twins in his lap, looked anxious. Baba stood before them, a twelve-year-old girl in a grubby golden tunic. Would they ever listen to her again?

Baba drew herself up and took a deep breath. "Yes, and you must trust me now, too."

She saw again the men walking away from Petronas. Their group had never been divided like this before. "My uncle . . ." she said, clasping her fingers tightly together. This was the hardest thing she'd ever had to say. "Ki was right. Four people now have caught the sleeping sickness. Other people might get sick, too."

There, she had said it. She saw Tulsi bow his head.

"I led you to water, yes, but I didn't look at anything else. All I saw was the water." The room was utterly silent, the people breathing as one. "If we stay here, more and more of us will get the sleeping sickness. Something strange is happening in this place – we do not belong here."

She looked at them all with her blue eye and her black eye. "We need to go – back to the desert. Back to what we know."

People were shuffling, murmuring.

Oh, grandmother, what would you have done?

Baba raised her head, suddenly sure of herself again. "There is no time to waste. We must go now – tonight."

Tonight!

Now!

The room erupted. Children jumped up and ran about. Old folk looked at each other in confusion. Yet the Baba had spoken. A hubbub filled the room. People were running out. Others were milling about, not sure what to do next.

Tulsi shuffled from foot to foot.

"Leave now?" he whispered.

Baba sighed. "Yes. It's the best thing. As soon as possible. I only hope it is soon enough."

Her father came over and hugged her. "I'm sorry it has come to this," said Kale, "but your grandmother would have been proud of you."

Baba's face went hot. "We will see," she murmured.

Baba hurried to her parents' house, where Anda still slept soundly on the mat. Baba had left Quirt to keep her company and the little creature was snuggled into her mother's neck. The room was starting to get dark, so Baba lit the lamp. Her mother looked the same. Baba knelt beside her and put a hand on her cool forehead. She felt a pang of guilt – or was it fear? Once they left Petronas, would her mother get better? If it was a spell, would it go away once they left this world?

"Don't worry, Mother," whispered Baba. "We are going home now."

The shadows were long and ghostly by the time people started gathering outside the meeting room with their rolled-up sleeping mats and pots and lamps. The rotobeasts had been herded together and now waited patiently while the tents were loaded onto the sleds. The goats had been roped together. The chickens were in their baskets. The children had been counted.

Tulsi struggled along with Baba's sleeping mat and his own over his shoulders. Two men carried the sleeping Anda on a stretcher. Merti and Tai were both on their feet now, being guided by family members. The largest man in the group carried Fas in his arms. The old man didn't make much of a bundle.

Baba clapped her hands. "Are we ready?"

"Yes, oh Baba."

A low humming seemed to be coming from the stone walls. Were they too late? Baba swallowed her fear. "Good," she said, trying to sound brave. "Then let us go – and quickly."

She led the way through alleys and courtyards

to the main entrance. It seemed such a long time ago that she first found this city – and now they were leaving.

Overhead, a whooshing sound made Baba look up. A black shape flew overhead. Beside her, Tulsi ducked. A child started wailing.

"What was that?" somebody cried.

"Thank the gods we are going!"

Baba hurried on. There was the yellow tree, dim now in the fading light. To her right was the short corridor that led to the archway. She stopped. Behind her, voices murmured.

"Why have we stopped? What's going on? What is happening?"

Baba swallowed. She looked at Tulsi. His eyes were wide with fright.

"The door has gone," she whispered.

Tulsi put down his load and hurried forward. Together, he and Baba patted the stone wall where once there had been an opening.

Kale joined them. "What is it?"

Baba stood back. "Petronas – it doesn't want us to leave."

chapter thirteen

They spent the rest of a miserable night huddled around the yellow tree. Nobody wanted to go back to their houses.

Meanwhile, Jad and some of the men worked on breaking a hole in the wall. Their blows echoed off the stone walls.

Baba sat on her mat, watching them. *It's not real*, she told herself. It was just like the flowers – magic. If she willed it hard enough, the wall might open up. When she tried, however, all that happened was a headache.

All around her, people were sleeping, snuffling, dreaming. Even Tulsi was curled up on his mat, fast asleep. The silent form of Baba's mother lay nearby. A breeze rustled through the leaves above the girl. It sounded like chuckling.

"Whatever you are," whispered Baba, "you are not going to win."

She must have dozed off. The sky was starting to grow light when Tulsi shook Baba awake.

"I've remembered something," he whispered. "Come on, I'll show you."

He led the way to the quiet corner where he had found the rope.

"What is it?" asked Baba, blinking up at the crossed sticks.

"Maybe it's our way out," said Tulsi. Bouncing up and down with excitement, he told her about the rope hanging on the other side of the wall and how it was secured. "At first I thought somebody had tried to get in – now I see it was the way they escaped."

"But how could they have escaped if the rope's on the outside?"

"Like this." Tulsi mimed throwing a rope up and then over a wall. "They would have taken turns to toss the rope over and climb down the other side."

Baba thought for a moment, frowning and silent. "Yes, but, Tulsi, the rope's on the other

side of the wall . . .”

“That’s okay,” he said quickly. “My father, he’s tall. He’ll be able to get the rope.”

Jad and some of the others stood looking up at the wall. Jad scratched his head. “It’s a long way up.”

“We could put somebody on your shoulders,” suggested someone.

“One of the women?”

“They can grab the sticks.”

“But what about the rotobeasts?” somebody asked.

“And the goats?”

Jad put his hand on Tulsi’s shoulder. “It was a good idea, son, but we can’t leave the animals.”

Tulsi’s face fell. “But what if we hauled them up – we could tie a rope around each rotobeast and pull it up and over.”

Two of the men exchanged a smile. The thought of a gangly rotobeast being hauled over the high wall was too much.

"I'm sorry, son," said Jad. Tulsi hung his head.

"He's right," murmured Baba. "We have to find some other way."

Baba sat by her sleeping mother, stroking her cold hand. Quirt was nestled in Anda's shoulder. The men were still working on the stone, and the bangs echoed loudly off the walls. So far, they'd only chipped off some bits of stone, and they were making so much noise. She glanced up at the sky and shivered. What if the bird came hurtling down at them?

Tulsi sat down beside her. He had brought a piece of flatbread, still warm from the fire.

"They won't be able to break through that stone," said Baba, biting into the bread.

"I don't think so, either."

They watched the men working. Every few minutes, Baba's father stopped to wipe his face. The wall was hardly scratched.

"You can't break magic that way," Baba muttered.

"True," said Tulsi, watching the men's tools bounce off the stone. "You have to fight magic with magic."

They sat on for a while in silence. Then Baba looked at the boy.

"What did you say?"

"Um, you have to fight magic with magic."

The girl's black and blue eyes gleamed. "Yes – but what kind of magic do *we* have?"

Tulsi shrugged. "I don't know."

"The way we live in the desert," said Baba. "Is there any magic in that?"

"Um . . ." Tulsi scratched his head, looking very like his father.

"What about the way we find the seeps?" said Baba.

Tulsi looked up. "Yes, with the water stick. That *is* a kind of magic, I suppose, but . . ."

"Of course it is," said Baba, getting up. "Come on."

"But where are we going?"

"To the tower – that's where all of this is coming from."

Baba scrabbled through her things and

pulled out the water stick. She ran her hands over the worn wood. The stick could find water, but what else could it do? What other power did the stick have? It was time to find out. She pushed back thoughts of her grandmother and the sand cat. Would it be safe?

Baba started running, with Tulsi close behind. They crossed canals and hurried through empty courtyards. They both knew where to go.

Then Baba turned a corner and suddenly stopped. Tulsi crashed into her.

"What is it?" he whispered.

"I must've taken a wrong turn," said Baba, puffing. "Don't know where I am."

Tulsi was looking around anxiously. "This way, I think."

Again they ran, and again they got lost. Tulsi looked frantically for his charcoal crosses. He ran back to the last courtyard they had been through. There was his mark on a wall, but he couldn't see any others.

"All this must be new," he gasped.

Baba shook her head in dismay. "It's really been growing."

At last, between two buildings, Tulsi glimpsed the top of the tower. "This way," he cried.

This time they walked, taking care to follow Tulsi's crosses. At each turning, there was now a new alleyway, a new direction to go.

"Do you think," asked Baba, "that the other door will still be open?"

"Probably not." Tulsi found another charcoal cross and led the way across a courtyard. "Everything's changed now. I don't even know how I'd find it again."

Suddenly, they were at the tower. They stood silently beneath it, looking up.

"Oh Baba, I am scared," Tulsi whispered.

"I'm scared, too," she said. The water stick felt heavy in her hands. She didn't even know what she was going to do with it. What if they . . . No, she didn't want to think about what might happen. "Come on," she said reluctantly.

"Yes, oh Baba," he murmured.

He followed the girl over to the dark door in the tower. Inside, it looked just as it had when Tulsi was there last: the dead leaves on the ground, the stone steps leading up into the gloom. A breathing silence came from within. Something else, too: a deep humming.

Baba's scarf started billowing. "Do you feel that?" she asked, looking back at Tulsi.

"Yes. It's like before a dust storm, when the wind picks up."

They looked at each other. Baba gripped the water stick more tightly, but still she hesitated, not wanting to go on. "We've only ever used the stick for finding water."

Tulsi's eyes were dark. "What else can we do, oh Baba?"

"Fight magic with magic," she whispered.

Baba stepped inside and slowly started up the steps. A chink of light came from above, showing the way. The steps spiralled upwards. On their right was empty space. Up and up they climbed, and the ground fell further away below them. Baba hugged the wall. The wind was getting stronger now.

Then something whooped past.

"What was that?" cried Tulsi.

Baba ducked low. "I couldn't see."

The wind was rising to a shriek. Baba's foot

slipped. She grabbed the wall on her left. The stone was smooth, but she used the stick to keep herself steady.

The light darkened, as if a cloud had passed in front of the sun and a harsh scream echoed in the tower. They crouched against the wall. Tulsi threw his arms over his head. He was shaking with fear.

Baba pushed herself forward, holding the stick out towards the drop. It was quivering and shaking. She had never felt it work like this before.

Again the light dimmed. "Look out!" cried Baba, crouching against the wall.

A long, hissing shadow raced towards them: sharp beak and black eyes.

Kereiya, it shrieked.

The stick started bucking in Baba's hands, as if it had found an enormous spring of water. The wind was fierce, but she hung onto it tightly. Her arms were aching.

"Help me hold it," she shouted.

Tulsi grabbed one end of the stick. It nearly lifted him off his feet.

"What's happening?" he cried.

"I can't see," shouted Baba.

The noise was huge now. A howling wind was crashing around the tower.

Then, suddenly, with a rushing howl, wings swept past them. It took all Baba's strength not to be swept off the steps.

"It's a monster," Tulsi shouted.

"No," shouted Baba. "It's only a bird!"

She fell to her knees. The wind was pulling her towards the edge. Tulsi grabbed her tunic.

"We have to get out," he cried.

Baba said something, but the wind sucked away her words. The stick was humming in her hands. Again, the bird swooped. The stick bucked. She could barely hold it. *Grandmother, help me!*

Then, over the sound of the wind, they heard a crack.

Tulsi's eyes were huge. "Run!" he screamed.

Down the steps they went – banging into each other, tumbling and crashing – and flung themselves out the door. When they turned to look back, they saw the stone shiver. Before their

eyes, a huge crack appeared in the tower.

Tulsi tugged at Baba's tunic. "Come *on*!" She scrambled to her feet and ran.

One glance back: the tower was crumbling. Stones were dashing to the ground. Dust billowed, and from the top of the tower wheeled a huge bird.

Kereiya, it shrieked.

Baba had one second to watch the bird flash up into the sky and vanish before Tulsi dragged her away.

They raced through the city with the sound of the tower crashing behind them.

"Hurry," cried Tulsi. "We don't have much time."

"What do you mean?" Baba panted.

The boy pointed at a bridge they had just crossed. There was a long crack in the stone. He didn't need to say anything more. The city was creaking and groaning around them. They hurried on.

When they reached the main courtyard, people were looking anxiously around them, or huddled in fearful groups. Children were crying. A high wind was tearing at the yellow tree and the water in the canal had been whipped up into foaming waves.

"Oh Baba," cried Shant. "Tell us what is happening."

But the girl raced past without stopping. She had to see the gate.

Jad, Kale and the others were standing back from the wall, where a huge crack had appeared. Chunks of stone had begun to fall to the ground and, with a groan, the wall teetered on the point of collapse.

Baba ran back to the group. "Hurry," she cried. "Get your things – get everybody out!" She ran over to her mother to fetch Quirt.

Ming was already pulling the goats. Others started hauling the rotobeasts forward by their ropes. Children ran out with bundles in their arms. Old folk carried pots and baskets. People shouldered rolled-up carpets. Kale and another man jogged through the opening, carrying

Anda's stretcher.

"The twins," her father shouted over his shoulder. Behind him, a woman grabbed the twins, one in each arm, and ran towards the opening.

The whole wall was crumbling now. Dust was flying. There was a loud noise as one of the nearby buildings crashed in on itself.

"Hurry," screamed Baba.

Out into the grasslands they went, as fast as they could. Behind them, Petronas was falling.

"Keep going," she cried. "Back to the desert!"

When she and Tulsi had put some distance between themselves and the city, Baba stopped, panting, and watched her fleeing people. One by one, they vanished into the grass. She saw the twins disappear, and the last of the rotobeasts. Now Baba turned back towards what was left of the walls. Petronas was collapsing. Far off in the distance came a single screech: *kereiya!*

Baba didn't wait any longer, but ran on into the long grass.

Suddenly, she lost her footing and landed on

hot sand. Quirt went flying. Then Tulsi came crashing down on top of her.

"Ow! Get off me!"

Tulsi rolled on his back, gasping. "We made it," he cried.

Baba sat up and looked around her. Quirt was running around in nervous circles. The twins were nearby, pink and screaming, her father trying to comfort them. One of the rotobeasts had got loose and it was romping away, with Jad running after it. People were all around – sitting on the sand, crying or hugging each other. It felt so good to feel the warm sand under her feet again. Above them, a hawk circled lazily in the blue sky.

"Yes, we made it."

"What happened, oh Baba?"

"I – I don't know," she muttered. Her hands were shaking. She looked at the water stick she was still holding. It didn't look anything special. Just a split branch from a tree. But something huge had happened. They could have been killed.

Baba looked at Tulsi, who was examining his

knee where he'd grazed it. She looked around at her people, her family. They had made it. They were home.

chapter fourteen

In her golden robe and fluttering red scarf, Baba was leading the way through the desert, holding the water stick between her hands. Bound to be water around here somewhere. She'd spotted two hawks in the distance, circling lazily in the sky. Probably after something – maybe a rabbit or a mouse. However, where there was a rabbit, there would be grasses, and where there was grass, no matter how brown and tough, there might be some water.

On her shoulder, Quirt was chittering nervously.

"Hush," murmured Baba. "The hawks won't get you."

This was a part of the desert they did not know. Low stony hills rose on their left. Cacti stood about like soldiers – plenty of cacti. They'd eat well that night. Baba smiled. As well as any desert prince.

"So, what do you think, Ki?"

The robed man stepped to her side, shading his eyes. Ever since he and the others had come back from the market town, Baba had made sure to ask his advice. In fact, she had found out that he knew a lot about finding water.

"I think, oh Baba, that we might find a seep down in that valley," he said, pointing ahead.

"Not up on that ridge, Ki?" she teased. "You know that sometimes we can find a seep on top of a hill."

He cleared his throat. "We could also look there, oh Baba, if you wish."

"You know," said Baba, "I think we shall."

They trudged up the hill. Stones skittered underfoot. At the top, she looked around, enjoying the view. In the distance, a smudge of smoke rose into the sky, marking the campsite. She had brought them back safely from Petronas. Her mother, Tai and Merti were back to normal. Fas still slept a lot, though he blamed that on his age. All in all, Baba felt pleased with herself. Life was good in the desert.

Their noise had startled a hare and it dashed away, zigzagging down the other side of the hill. Baba shaded her eyes with her hand and squinted into the distance. Wasn't that . . .

"Tulsi," she called.

The boy jogged up beside her. "Yes, oh Baba?"

"What do you see over there?"

The boy looked and grinned. "It is a mirage, oh Baba."

Baba was also grinning. "You know, I think we are looking at something green."

"If it is not a mirage . . ." said Tulsi.

". . . then there will be water," said Baba.

And, so saying, she flipped the end of her red scarf over her shoulder and hurried forward.